FASCINATING BOGOTÁ
2024

A Practical Traveler's Guide to Exploring Columbia's High-Altitude Capital

KRUYS TRAVIS

Disclaimer:

The information provided in this travel guide is for general informational purposes only. While every effort has been made to ensure the accuracy and completeness of the content, the publisher and authors make no representations or warranties, express or implied, regarding the accuracy, suitability, or availability of the information contained herein.

The travel recommendations, tips, and suggestions are based on the authors' experiences and research at the time of publication. However, travel conditions, regulations, and services may change, and it is the responsibility of the reader to verify any information independently before relying on it.

The publisher and authors disclaim any liability for any loss, injury, or inconvenience incurred by individuals or entities using the information provided in this guide. Travelers are urged to exercise due diligence and make their own judgments regarding safety, health, and travel conditions.

All product and company names mentioned in this guide are trademarks or registered trademarks of their respective owners. Reference to any specific commercial product, process, or service does not constitute or imply endorsement or recommendation by the publisher.

Please check with relevant authorities and official sources for the most up-to-date information on travel destinations, regulations, and safety guidelines.

TABLE OF CONTENTS

INTRODUCTION

Hi there, and welcome to this travel guide to Bogotá, Colombia. I'm so excited to share with you one of my favorite cities in the world, and I hope you'll love it as much as I do. Bogotá is a city of contrasts and surprises, where you'll find a blend of history, culture, nature, and adventure. Whether you're a first-time visitor or a seasoned traveler, Bogotá has something for you.

In this book, I'll show you the best things to see and do in Bogotá, as well as some tips and tricks to make the most of your trip. You'll learn about the top attractions, the hidden gems, the food and drink, the culture and arts, the shopping and markets, the nature and sports, and the day trips and excursions. You'll also get some practical information on how to get there and get around, how to stay safe and healthy, and how to speak some basic Spanish.

This book is designed to help you plan your trip according to your interests, preferences, and budget. You can use this book as a reference, a guide, or a companion. You can read it from cover to cover, or skip to the chapters that interest you the most. You can follow the suggested itineraries, or create your own. You can use the maps, photos, icons, and symbols to help you navigate the city and find what you're looking for. You can also use the websites, apps, books, and contacts to get more information and resources.

Bogotá is a city that will challenge your expectations and reward your curiosity. It will make you feel alive and connected. Bogotá will make you fall in love with it. So, are you ready to visit Bogotá? Let's go!

1

BOGOTÀ BASICS: WHAT YOU NEED TO KNOW BEFORE YOU GO

Before you pack your bags and head to Bogotá, there are some things you need to know to prepare for your trip. In this chapter, I'll give you some basic information about the geography, climate, history, culture, facts, figures, transportation, accommodation, safety, health, and language of Bogotá. This will help you get a better understanding of the city and what to expect when you arrive.

GEOGRAPHY AND CLIMATE

Bogotá is located in the center of Colombia, on a high plateau called the Bogotá savanna, at an altitude of about 2,600 meters (8,500 feet) above sea level. Bogotá is surrounded by mountains, rivers, and forests, and has a variety of landscapes and ecosystems. Bogotá is the largest and most populous city in Colombia, with an area of 1,587 square kilometers (613 square miles) and a population of about 8 million people.

Bogotá has a subtropical highland climate, which means that it has mild temperatures throughout the year, with an average of 14°C (57°F). However, Bogotá also has a lot of microclimates, which means that the weather can vary depending on the location, elevation, and time of the day. Bogotá has two rainy seasons, from April to June and from September to November, and two dry seasons, from December to March and from July to August. Bogotá can be sunny, cloudy, rainy, windy, or foggy, sometimes all in the same day. So, it's always a good idea to dress in layers and bring an umbrella or a raincoat.

HISTORY AND CULTURE

Bogotá has a long and rich history, dating back to the pre-Columbian times, when it was inhabited by the Muisca people, who had a complex and advanced civilization. Bogotá was founded in 1538 by the Spanish conquistador Gonzalo Jimenez de Quesada, who named it Santa Fe de Bogotá, after his hometown in Spain. Bogotá became the capital of the New Kingdom of Granada, and later of the Viceroyalty of New Granada, which included present-day Colombia, Venezuela, Ecuador, Panama, and parts of Peru and Brazil. Bogotá was the center of the independence movement against the Spanish rule, led by Simon Bolivar, who liberated Colombia and other countries in 1819. Bogotá became the capital of the Republic of Colombia, and has been the scene of many political, social, and cultural events that have shaped the country's history.

Bogotá's history and culture are shaped by the influences of the indigenous Muisca people, the Spanish colonizers, the independence heroes, and the contemporary social movements. The Muisca were a complex civilization that inhabited the Bogotá savanna before the arrival of the Spanish in the 16th century. They had a sophisticated political and religious system, based on the dual leadership of the zipa and the zaque, and the worship of the sun and the moon. The Spanish founded the city of Santa Fé de Bogotá in 1538, on the site of the Muisca capital of Bacatá. They imposed their language, religion, and laws, but also mixed with the native and African populations, creating a mestizo culture. Bogotá was the seat of the Viceroyalty of New Granada, and the center of the independence movement led by Simón Bolívar and his followers. After independence, Bogotá became the capital of the Republic of Colombia, and witnessed many political and social changes, such as the civil wars, the La Violencia period, the drug wars, and the peace process. Bogotá is also a city of art, literature, music, and gastronomy, with famous figures such as Fernando Botero, Gabriel García Márquez, Shakira, and Juan Valdez.

Bogotá has a diverse and vibrant culture, influenced by its indigenous, European, African, and mestizo heritage. Bogotá is known for its music, dance, art, literature, and festivals, as well as its cuisine, architecture, and fashion. Bogotá is also a melting pot of people from different regions, backgrounds, and lifestyles, who coexist in harmony and tolerance. Bogotá is a city that celebrates its diversity and creativity, and welcomes visitors with open arms.

FACTS AND FIGURES

Bogotá is the capital and largest city of Colombia, as well as the political, economic, cultural, and educational center of the country. Bogotá is also one of the most important cities in

Latin America, and a major hub for business, trade, tourism, and innovation. Here are some facts and figures about Bogotá:

- Bogotá is the third-highest capital city in the world, after La Paz and Quito.
- Bogotá is the fourth-most populous city in South America, after Sao Paulo, Lima, and Buenos Aires.
- Bogotá is the home of the largest and oldest university in Colombia, the National University of Colombia, founded in 1867.
- Bogotá is the home of the largest and most visited museum in Colombia, the Gold Museum, which has more than 55,000 pieces of pre-Columbian gold.
- Bogotá is the home of the largest and most famous street art festival in the world, the Bogotá Graffiti Festival, which attracts more than 300 artists from 30 countries every year.
- Bogotá is the home of the largest and most spectacular flower market in the world, the Flower Market of Paloquemao, which sells more than 50,000 flowers every day.
- Bogotá is the home of the largest and most popular bike path network in Latin America, the Ciclovia, which covers more than 120 kilometers (75 miles) and attracts more than 2 million people every Sunday and holiday.

Bogotá is well-connected to the rest of the world, and has many options for transportation. Here are some ways to get to and around Bogotá:

- **By Plane**: Bogotá has one international airport, the El Dorado International Airport, which is located about 15 kilometers (9 miles) west of the city center. The airport has flights to and from more than 50 destinations in America, Europe, and Asia, and is served by more than 30 airlines. The airport has two terminals, one for domestic flights and one for international flights, and has many facilities and services, such as shops, restaurants, banks, ATMs, currency exchange, Wi-Fi, luggage storage, and car rental. You have three options for transportation from the airport to the city: bus, shuttle, or taxi. A taxi will cost you about 30,000 pesos (about 8 USD), a bus will cost you about 2,000 pesos (about 0.5 USD), and a shuttle will cost you about 15,000 pesos (about 4 USD).

- **By Bus**: Bogotá has two main bus terminals, the Terminal de Transporte de Bogotá, which is located in the west of the city, and the Terminal de Transporte del Sur, which is located in the south of the city. The bus terminals have connections to and from more than 1,000 destinations in Colombia and neighboring countries, and are served by more than 100 bus companies. The bus terminals have many facilities and services, such as shops, restaurants, banks, ATMs, currency exchange, Wi-Fi, luggage storage, and car rental. To get from the bus terminals to the city, you can take a taxi, a bus, or a metro. A taxi will cost you about 20,000 pesos (about 5 USD), a bus will cost you about 2,000 pesos (about 0.5 USD), and a metro will cost you about 2,400 pesos (about 0.6 USD).

- **By Car**: Bogotá has a network of roads and highways that connect it to the rest of the country and the region. The main highways are the Autopista Norte, which goes to the north of the country, the Autopista Sur, which goes to the south of the country, the Autopista Medellin, which goes to the west of the country, and the Autopista al Llano, which goes to the east of the country. The highways have tolls, which vary depending on the distance and the vehicle type. To drive in Bogotá, you need a valid driver's license, a vehicle registration, and an insurance. You can rent a car at the airport, the bus terminals, or the city center, from various car rental companies. The average price for renting a car is about 150,000 pesos (about 40 USD) per day, plus gas and tolls. Driving in Bogotá can be challenging, due to the traffic, the pollution, the road conditions, and the driving habits of the locals. You also need to be aware of the Pico y Placa, which is a restriction that limits the circulation of vehicles based on their license plate number and the day of the week, to reduce congestion and emissions.

- **By Metro**: Bogotá has a metro system, called the Transmilenio, which is a bus rapid transit system that operates on dedicated lanes and stations. The Transmilenio covers more than 100 kilometers (62 miles) and has 12 lines and 139 stations, that connect the main areas of the city. The Transmilenio runs from 4 a.m. to 11 p.m. on weekdays, and from 5 a.m. to 10 p.m. on weekends and holidays. To use the Transmilenio, you need to buy a smart card, called the TuLlave, which costs 5,000 pesos (about 1.3 USD) and can be recharged at any station. The fare for the Transmilenio is 2,400 pesos (about 0.6 USD) per trip, regardless of the distance or the number of transfers. The Transmilenio is fast, cheap, and convenient, but it can also be crowded, noisy, and unsafe, especially during peak hours and at night. You need to be careful with your belongings and your personal space, and avoid the stations and buses that are marked as high-risk or dangerous.

- **By Bike**: Bogotá has a bike culture, and has many options for cycling. Bogotá has more than 550 kilometers (340 miles) of bike paths, called the Ciclorutas, which cover the main streets and avenues of the city. Bogotá also has a bike sharing system, called the Bici, which has more than 6,000 bikes and 500 stations, that are free to use for up to an hour. Bogotá also has a bike event, called the Ciclovia, which closes more than 120 kilometers (75 miles) of roads to cars and opens them to bikes, skates, and pedestrians, every Sunday and holiday, from 7 a.m. to 2 p.m. Bogotá also has many bike shops, bike tours, bike clubs, and bike events, that cater to all kinds of cyclists. Cycling in Bogotá is fun, healthy, and eco-friendly, but it can also be risky, due to the traffic, the pollution, the road conditions, and the crime. You need to be careful with your bike and your belongings, and follow the rules and signs. You also need to wear a helmet, a reflective vest, and a light, especially at night.

Bogotá has a wide range of accommodations to suit every taste, budget, and need. You can choose from hotels, hostels, apartments, guesthouses, bed and breakfasts, and more. You can also find different styles, locations, and amenities, depending on what you're looking for. Here are some tips to help you find the best accommodation for you:

- If you want to stay in the center of the action, look for accommodations in La Candelaria, Chapinero, or Zona Rosa, which are the most popular and lively areas of the city. You'll find many attractions, restaurants, bars, and shops within walking distance, as well as easy access to public transportation. However, these areas can also be noisy, crowded, and expensive, so you may want to look for a quieter and cheaper option if you prefer.

- If you want to stay in a more residential and relaxed area, look for accommodations in Usaquen, Teusaquillo, or Suba, which are the more suburban and green areas of the city. You'll find more space, comfort, and tranquility, as well as some local charm and hidden gems. However, these areas can also be far from the main attractions, and you may need to take a taxi, a bus, or a metro to get to the city center.

- If you want to stay in a more alternative and creative area, look for accommodations in La Macarena, San Felipe, or Ciudad Bolivar, which are the more artistic and cultural areas of the city. You'll find more street art, galleries, museums, and festivals, as well as some social and environmental projects and initiatives. However, these areas can also be less developed, less safe, and less comfortable, so you may want to do some research and be careful before booking.

- If you want to stay in a more luxurious and exclusive area, look for accommodations in Rosales, Chico, or Santa Barbara, which are the most upscale and elegant areas of the city. You'll find more high-end hotels, restaurants, shops, and services, as well as some beautiful parks and views. However, these areas can also be very expensive, very isolated, and very boring, so you may want to look for a more authentic and fun option if you can.

No matter what kind of accommodation you choose, make sure to check the reviews, ratings, photos, and descriptions before booking. You can use websites like Booking.com, Airbnb.com, or Hostelworld.com to compare and book your accommodation online. You can also use apps like HotelTonight, Couchsurfing, or Booking Now to find last-minute deals, free couches, or instant bookings. The average price for accommodation in Bogotá is about 100,000 pesos (about 27 USD) per night, but it can vary depending on the season, the location, and the quality.

STAYING SAFE AND HEALTHY

Bogotá is a safe and healthy city, as long as you follow some common sense and precaution. Bogotá has improved a lot in terms of security and sanitation in the past years, and most tourists have a positive and trouble-free experience. However, Bogotá is still a big and complex city, and it has some issues and risks that you need to be aware of and avoid. Here are some tips to help you stay safe and healthy in Bogotá:

- Be careful with your belongings and your personal space, especially in crowded and touristy areas, such as La Candelaria, Plaza Bolivar, or the Transmilenio stations and buses. Like every big city, there are a lot of pickpockets, scammers, and thieves, who can target unsuspecting and distracted tourists. Don't carry too much cash, valuables, or documents, and keep them in a safe and hidden place. Don't flaunt your phone, camera, or jewelry, and don't leave them unattended. Don't accept any offers, gifts, or drinks from strangers, and don't trust anyone who seems too friendly or helpful.

- Be careful with your transportation and your destination, especially at night, in remote or unfamiliar areas, or when using taxis, buses, or metros. Bogotá has a lot of traffic, pollution, and road accidents, which can make traveling in the city stressful and dangerous. Don't walk alone, in the dark, or in the wrong direction, and always check the map and the address before you go. Don't take any taxi, bus, or metro that looks suspicious, old, or unlicensed, and always check the meter, the route, and the fare before you get in. Don't go to any place that looks sketchy, empty, or unsafe, and always ask for recommendations, directions, and opinions from locals or other travelers.

- Be careful with your health and your body, especially if you have any allergies, conditions, or sensitivities, or if you're not used to the altitude, the climate, or the food. Bogotá has a lot of pollution, germs, and diseases, which can affect your health and well-being. Don't drink tap water, and only drink bottled or filtered water. Don't eat street food, and only eat cooked or peeled food. Don't drink too much alcohol, and only drink in moderation and with people you trust. Don't do any drugs, and only do them if you know what they are and what they do. Don't have any unprotected sex, and only have sex with people you know and trust.

Bogotá is a safe and healthy city, as long as you follow these common sense and precaution. If you have any problems, questions, or emergencies, you can always ask for help from the police, the hospital, the embassy, or the hotel. You can also use apps like Uber, Google Maps, or WhatsApp to get a ride, find your way, or communicate with someone. The emergency number in Bogotá is 123, and the police number is 112.

SPEAKING SPANISH

Bogotá is a Spanish-speaking city, and most people in Bogotá speak Spanish as their first or only language. Spanish is the official and dominant language of Colombia, and it has some variations and accents that are unique to the country and the region. Bogotá has a neutral and clear accent, which is easy to understand and learn. However, Bogotá also has some slang, expressions, and words that are specific to the city and the culture. Here are some tips to help you speak Spanish in Bogotá:

- Learn some basic Spanish before you go, or take some Spanish classes when you arrive. Spanish is a beautiful and useful language, and learning some Spanish will make your trip more enjoyable and rewarding. You'll be able to communicate with the locals, understand the signs and menus, and appreciate the culture and history. You can use websites like Duolingo.com, Babbel.com, or Busuu.com to learn some Spanish online. You can also use apps like Google Translate, SpanishDict, or WordReference to translate some words or phrases. You can also take some Spanish classes in Bogotá, from various schools, teachers, or exchanges. The average price for a Spanish class in Bogotá is about 30,000 pesos (about 8 USD) per hour, but it can vary depending on the level, the location, and the quality.

- Speak slowly, clearly, and politely, and don't be afraid to ask for repetition, clarification, or help. Bogotá is a friendly and welcoming city, and most people in Bogotá are willing and happy to help you with your Spanish. Don't be shy, embarrassed, or frustrated, and try to speak as much as you can. Don't worry about making mistakes, and learn from them. Don't speak too fast, too loud, or too slangy, and try to speak as clearly and as politely as you can. Don't hesitate to ask for repetition, clarification, or help, and use phrases like "¿Puede repetir, por favor?" (Can you repeat, please?), "¿Qué significa esto?" (What does this mean?), or "¿Me puede ayudar?" (Can you help me?).

- Learn some slang, expressions, and words that are specific to Bogotá, and use them with caution and context. Bogotá has a rich and colorful language, and learning some slang, expressions, and words that are specific to Bogotá will make your trip more fun and authentic. You'll be able to understand the jokes, the references, and the nuances, and you'll be able to connect with the locals and the culture. However, you also need to be careful and respectful, and use them with caution and context. Some slang, expressions, and words can be offensive, rude, or inappropriate, depending on the situation, the tone, and the person. Here are some examples of slang, expressions, and words that are specific to Bogotá, and their meanings:

- *"¿Qué más?" (What else?): This is a common and casual way to greet someone or start a conversation. It means "What's up?" or "How are you?".*
- *"Bacano" (Cool): This is a common and positive way to describe something or someone that is cool, awesome, or amazing. It can also be used as an interjection, like "Wow!" or "Great!".*
- *"Parce" (Buddy): This is a common and friendly way to address someone or refer to someone that is your friend, buddy, or mate. It can also be used as a term of endearment, like "Dude" or "Pal".*

- *"Chévere" (Nice): This is a common and versatile way to express approval, satisfaction, or agreement. It means "Nice", "Good", or "OK".*

Bogotá has a rich and colorful language, and learning some slang, expressions, and words that are specific to Bogotá will make your trip more fun and authentic. You'll be able to understand the jokes, the references, and the nuances, and you'll be able to connect with the locals and the culture. However, you also need to be careful and respectful, and use them with caution and context. Some slang, expressions, and words can be offensive, rude, or inappropriate, depending on the situation, the tone, and the person. Here are some examples of slang, expressions, and words that are specific to Bogotá, and their meanings:

- *"Ojo" (Eye): This is a common and useful way to warn someone or draw their attention to something. It means "Watch out", "Be careful", or "Look".*
- *"Guayabo" (Guava): This is a common and funny way to describe the feeling of having a hangover. It means "Hangover".*
- *"Rumbear" (To rumble): This is a common and fun way to describe the act of going out, partying, or dancing. It means "To party".*

- *"Chanda" (Cheap): This is a common and negative way to describe something or someone that is low-quality, poor, or stingy. It means "Cheap", "Lousy", or "Miserly".*
- *"Berraco" (Fierce): This is a common and positive way to describe something or someone that is strong, brave, or determined. It means "Fierce", "Tough", or "Awesome".*
- *"Mamera" (Suck): This is a common and expressive way to describe something or someone that is boring, annoying, or tedious. It means "Suck", "Bore", or "Drag".*

YOUR 7-DAY ITINERARY

DAY 1: ARRIVAL AND CITY TOUR

- Arrive at El Dorado International Airport and take a taxi or a bus to your hotel. You can choose from a variety of accommodation options, from budget hostels to luxury hotels.

- After checking in and resting, you can start exploring the city by taking a walking tour of La Candelaria, the historic center of Bogotá. You can visit the Plaza de Bolívar, the Primatial Cathedral of Bogotá[1], the Palace of Justice, and the Capitolio Nacional.
- You can also visit some of the museums in the area, such as the Gold Museum[2], which displays thousands of gold artifacts from the pre-Columbian era, and the Botero Museum, which showcases the works of the famous Colombian artist Fernando Botero.
- For lunch, you can try some of the local dishes, such as ajiaco (a chicken and potato soup), bandeja paisa (a platter of rice, beans, meat, eggs, and plantains), or arepas (corn cakes with cheese or meat).
- In the afternoon, you can take a cable car or a funicular to the top of Monserrate, a hill that offers a panoramic view of the city. You can also visit the church and the sanctuary on the hill, which are popular pilgrimage sites.
- For dinner, you can enjoy the nightlife of Bogotá by going to one of the many restaurants, bars, or clubs in the Zona Rosa or the Zona G, two of the city's most vibrant and trendy areas.

Options And Alternatives:

- If you are interested in street art, you can take a graffiti tour of Bogotá and learn about the history, culture, and politics behind the colorful murals and tags.
- If you are a fan of literature, you can visit the house of Gabriel García Márquez, the Nobel Prize-winning author of One Hundred Years of Solitude and other magical realism novels.
- If you want to experience the local culture, you can join a salsa or cumbia class and learn how to dance to the rhythms of Colombia.

DAY 2: MUSEUMS AND PARKS

- After breakfast, you can spend the day visiting some of the museums and parks that Bogotá has to offer.
- You can start with the National Museum of Colombia, the oldest and largest museum in the country, which displays the history, culture, and art of Colombia from the pre-Columbian times to the present day.
- You can then visit the Maloka Interactive Center, a science and technology museum that features interactive exhibits, games, and simulations that are fun and educational for all ages.
- For lunch, you can go to the Usaquén district, a charming area that has a colonial-style architecture and a variety of restaurants, cafés, and shops.

- In the afternoon, you can visit the Simon Bolivar Park, the largest and most popular park in Bogotá, which has a lake, a sports complex, a concert venue, and a children's playground. You can also visit the Bogotá Botanical Garden, which has a collection of plants from different regions of Colombia and the world.
- For dinner, you can go to the Parque de la 93, a trendy and modern area that has a wide range of restaurants, bars, and clubs to suit your taste and mood.

Options And Alternatives:

- If you are interested in art, you can visit the Museum of Modern Art of Bogotá, which has a collection of works by Colombian and international artists from the 20th and 21st centuries.
- If you are a fan of sports, you can watch a soccer match at the El Campín Stadium, the home of the Bogotá teams Santa Fe and Millonarios.
- If you want to experience the local culture, you can join a tejo game, a traditional sport that involves throwing metal discs at a clay target with gunpowder.

DAY 3: ZIPAQUIRA: SALT MINE & SALT CATHEDRAL TOUR

- After breakfast, you can take a day trip to Zipaquira, a town that is about an hour away from Bogotá by car or bus.

- In Zipaquira, you can visit the Salt Cathedral, a stunning underground church that was carved out of a salt mine. You can admire the sculptures, the altars, and the lighting effects that create a mystical atmosphere.
- You can also visit the Salt Park, a theme park that showcases the history, culture, and industry of salt mining in Colombia. You can see the machinery, the tunnels, and the exhibitions that explain the process and the importance of salt.
- For lunch, you can try some of the regional specialties, such as fritanga (a mix of fried meats and potatoes), cuchuco (a thick soup of wheat, potatoes, and meat), or almojábanas (cheese breads).
- In the afternoon, you can return to Bogotá and relax at your hotel or explore more of the city.

- **Options And Alternatives:**

- If you are interested in nature, you can visit the Chicaque Natural Park, a cloud forest reserve that has trails, waterfalls, and wildlife.
- If you are a fan of history, you can visit the Nemocón Salt Mine, another salt mine that has a museum, a movie set, and a crystal chamber with a giant salt crystal.
- If you want to experience the local culture, you can visit the Guatavita Lake, a sacred site for the indigenous Muisca

people, who performed rituals and offerings of gold to their god. This lake is also the origin of the legend of El Dorado, the mythical city of gold that attracted many Spanish explorers.

DAY 4: SHOPPING AND ENTERTAINMENT

- After breakfast, you can spend the day shopping and enjoying the entertainment options that Bogotá has to offer.
- You can start with the Hacienda Santa Barbara, a former colonial estate that has been converted into a shopping mall that has a mix of local and international brands, as well as a cinema, a food court, and a cultural center.
- You can then visit the Unicentro, one of the largest and most modern shopping malls in Bogotá, which has over 300 stores, a supermarket, a casino, a bowling alley, and a multiplex cinema.
- For lunch, you can go to the Salitre Plaza, another shopping mall that has a variety of restaurants, cafés, and fast food outlets.
- In the afternoon, you can visit the Salitre Magico, an amusement park that has rides, games, and shows for all ages. You can also visit the Mundo Aventura, another amusement park that has a zoo, a water park, and a 4D cinema.

- For dinner, you can go to the Corferias, a convention center that hosts events, exhibitions, and festivals throughout the year. You can also go to the Teatro Mayor Julio Mario Santo Domingo, a theater that showcases performances of music, dance, theater, and opera.

- **Options And Alternative**s:

- If you are interested in crafts, you can visit the Usaquén Flea Market, a weekly market that sells handmade products, antiques, and souvenirs.
- If you are a fan of movies, you can visit the Cinemateca Distrital, a cultural center that screens independent, alternative, and classic films.
- If you want to experience the local culture, you can visit the Plaza de Mercado de Paloquemao, a traditional market that sells fresh fruits, vegetables, flowers, and meats.

DAY 5: LA CHORRERA AND LA CALERA

- After breakfast, you can take another day trip to La Chorrera and La Calera, two natural attractions that are about an hour away from Bogotá by car or bus.
- In La Chorrera, you can hike to the La Chorrera Waterfall, the highest waterfall in Colombia, with a height of 590 meters (1,936 feet). You can enjoy the scenery, the flora and fauna, and the fresh air of the Andean forest.

- In La Calera, you can visit the Mirador de La Calera, a viewpoint that offers a spectacular view of Bogotá and the surrounding mountains. You can also enjoy a cup of coffee or a snack at one of the cafés or restaurants nearby.
- For lunch, you can have a picnic at the park or try some of the local delicacies, such as trucha (trout), changua (a milk and egg soup), or masato (a fermented rice drink).
- In the afternoon, you can return to Bogotá and relax at your hotel or explore more of the city.

- **Options And Alternatives:**

- If you are interested in adventure, you can do some paragliding, rappelling, or zip-lining at the Suesca Rocks, a rock formation that is popular for outdoor activities.
- If you are a fan of culture, you can visit the Guatavita New Town, a picturesque village that was relocated after the original town was flooded by the construction of a dam.
- If you want to experience the local culture, you can visit the Choachí Hot Springs, a thermal spa that has pools, saunas, and massages.

DAY 6: FREE DAY

- After breakfast, you can have a free day to do whatever you want in Bogotá. You can revisit some of the places that you liked, discover new ones, or take an optional tour to a nearby destination, such as Villa de Leyva, Chicaque, or Suesca.

- For lunch and dinner, you can choose from the many options that Bogotá has to offer, or try something different, such as fusion cuisine, vegetarian food, or ethnic food.

DAY 7: DEPARTURE

- After breakfast, you can check out from your hotel and take a taxi or a bus to the airport. You can also do some last-minute shopping or sightseeing before your flight. You can say goodbye to Bogotá and hope to return soon.

2

BOGOTÁ HIGHLIGHTS: THE BEST OF THE BEST IN BOGOTÁ

Bogotá is a city full of amazing sights and attractions, and it can be hard to choose what to see and do. That's why I've created this list of the best of the best in Bogotá, the highlights that you can't miss. These are the places that will make you fall in love with Bogotá, and give you a taste of its history, culture, nature, and art:

LA CANDELARIA

Address: Calle 10 # 0 15 Bogotá, Colombia.
Rating: 4.5 out of 5 based on 4774 reviews

This is the historic heart of Bogotá, where the city was founded in 1538. La Candelaria is a colorful and charming neighborhood, full of colonial buildings, cobblestone streets, and hidden plazas. La Candelaria is also a cultural hub, where you can find many museums, galleries, theaters, and libraries. Some of the most important attractions in La Candelaria are the Gold Museum, the Botero Museum, the Plaza Bolivar, and the Cathedral. La Candelaria is a place where you can feel the spirit and the history of Bogotá, and where you can admire its beauty and architecture.

MONSERRATE

Address: Cra. 2 Este #41-48, Bogotá, Colombia.
Rating :4.5 out of 5 based on 484 reviews

This is the mountain that overlooks the city, and that offers the best views of Bogotá. Monserrate dominates the skyline of Bogotá, and that offers the most breathtaking views of the city and its surroundings. From the top of Monserrate, you can see the contrast between the modern skyscrapers and the colonial buildings, the green hills and the urban sprawl, and the snow-capped mountains and the tropical plains. Monserrate is more than just a viewpoint, it is also a sacred place for the locals, who visit it for religious and spiritual reasons. Many people climb to Monserrate to pray, to make vows, or to thank God for their blessings. Monserrate has a church, a sanctuary, and a statue of the Fallen Christ, which are symbols of the faith and the devotion of Bogotá. The church, built in the 17th century, has a baroque style and a wooden altar. The sanctuary, built in the 20th century, has a modern style and a glass dome. The statue of the Fallen Christ, made of wood and covered with gold, is said to have miraculous powers and to grant wishes. Monserrate also has a park, a garden, and some restaurants, where you can relax and have a bite. The park, located behind the church, has a fountain, a pond, and a cross. The garden, located in front of the sanctuary, has flowers, trees, and benches. The restaurants, located on the sides of the mountain, have local and international cuisine, and panoramic views. Monserrate is a place where you can appreciate the beauty and the magnitude of Bogotá, and where you can feel closer to the sky and to God. You can reach Monserrate by cable car, by funicular, or by hiking. The cable car, also known as the teleférico, is a fast and comfortable way to get to the top, and it operates from 6am to 11:30pm on weekdays, and from 5:30am to 11:30pm on weekends and holidays. The funicular, also known as the tranvía, is a slow and scenic way to get to the top, and it operates from 6:30am to 11:30pm on weekdays, and from 5:30am to 11:30pm on weekends and holidays. The hiking, also known as the caminata, is a challenging and rewarding way to get to the top, and it takes about an hour and a half, but it is only recommended during the day and with a local guide, as the trail can be steep and unsafe.

THE GOLD MUSEUM

Address: Carrera 6 No.15-88, Bogotá, Colombia.
Rating: 4.5 out of 5 based on 14562 reviews.

The Gold Museum is one of the most popular and fascinating attractions in Bogotá, Colombia. It is located in the historic center of the city, near the Parque de Santander and the Plaza de Bolívar. The Gold Museum is part of the cultural network of the Banco de la República, the central bank of Colombia, which also manages other museums and libraries in the country.

The Gold Museum was founded In 1939, when the Banco de la República acquired the first piece of its collection, the Poporo Quimbaya, a gold vessel used by the Quimbaya people for their coca rituals. Since then, the museum has grown to include more than 55,000 pieces of gold, silver, and copper, as well as pottery, stone, wood, and textile objects that represent the different cultures that inhabited Colombia before the Spanish conquest. The museum has the largest collection of pre-Columbian gold in the world, and it is recognized as a national and international cultural heritage.

The Gold Museum displays Its collection in four exhibition rooms, each with a different theme and approach. The first room is called "Working Metals", and it explains the techniques and processes used by the pre-Columbian goldsmiths to create their objects, such as hammering, casting, soldering, and alloying. The second room is called "People and Gold in pre-Hispanic Colombia", and it presents the geographical and cultural diversity of Colombia, and the different uses and meanings of gold for the indigenous peoples, such as adornment, ritual, power, and trade. The third room is called "Cosmology and Symbolism", and it explores the worldview and beliefs of the pre-Columbian cultures, and the symbols and representations of gold in their cosmogony, mythology, and spirituality. The fourth room is called "The Offering", and it recreates the ceremony of the offering of gold to the gods, which was performed by some cultures, such as the Muisca, in sacred lakes or temples. The room has a circular shape, and it uses light and sound effects to create a sensory and immersive experience.

The Gold Museum Is a place where you can discover and appreciate the richness and diversity of the pre-Columbian cultures of Colombia, and the beauty and value of their gold work. The museum also offers guided tours, audio guides, workshops, publications, and temporary exhibitions, to enhance your visit and learning. The museum is open from Tuesday to Saturday, from 9am to 6pm, and on Sundays, from 10 a.m. to 4 p.m. The entrance fee is 4,000 COP (1.14 USD) for adults, and free for children, students, and seniors. On Sundays, everyone can enter for free. The museum also has a shop, a restaurant, and a library.

BOTERO MUSEUM

Address: Calle 11 No.4-41, Bogotá, Colombia.
Rating: 4.5 out of 5 based on 10479 reviews
This is the residence of Fernando Botero, a well-known Colombian artist noted for his paintings and sculptures featuring exaggerated and sensual bodies. The Botero

Museum has more than 200 works of art, donated by Botero himself, that represent his style and his vision of the world. The Botero Museum also has a collection of works by other renowned artists, such as Picasso, Monet, Dali, and Matisse, that Botero admired and collected. The Botero Museum is a place where you can enjoy the art and the humor of Botero, and where you can discover his influences and his inspirations.

PLAZA BOLIVAR

Address: Between Carreras 7 and 8 at Calle 10, Bogotá, Colombia.
Rating: 4 out of 5 based on 3482 reviews

This is the main square and political center of Bogotá, and the scene of many historical and social events. Plaza Bolivar is surrounded by some of the most important buildings of the city, such as the Cathedral, the Palace of Justice, the Capitol, and the Mayor's Office. Plaza Bolivar also has a statue of Simon Bolivar, the liberator of Colombia and other countries, and a symbol of the independence and the identity of Bogotá. Plaza Bolivar is a place where you can witness the history and the politics of Bogotá, and where you can join the crowds and the pigeons that fill the square.

NATIONAL MUSEUM OF COLOMBIA

The National Museum of Colombia is one of the most important and interesting attractions in Bogotá, Colombia. It is located in the historic center of the city, near the Parque de Santander and the Plaza de Bolívar. The National Museum of Colombia is part of the cultural network of the Banco de la República, the central bank of Colombia, which also manages other museums and libraries in the country.

The National Museum of Colombia was founded In 1823, making it the oldest museum in the country and one of the oldest in the continent. The museum is housed in a building that was originally a prison, built in 1874. The building has a fortress-like architecture, with stone and brick walls, arches, domes, and columns. The building has a Greek cross shape, with 104 cells distributed around a central courtyard. The building served as a prison until 1946, when it was adapted for the museum. The building was restored and renovated in 1975, and again in 2000. The building is a national monument and a symbol of the history and the identity of Colombia.

The National Museum of Colombia ha" a collection of more than 20,000 objects that represent the history, the culture, the art, and the society of Colombia, from the pre-Columbian times to the present day. The collection includes archaeological and ethnographic artifacts, historical documents and photographs, paintings and sculptures, textiles and costumes, musical instruments and recordings, and everyday objects and memorabilia. The collection is organized in four exhibition rooms, each with a different theme and approach. The first room is called "The Nation: Symbols and Rituals", and it explores the formation and the evolution of the Colombian nation, through its symbols, rituals, and institutions. The second room is called "The Nation: Memory and Violence", and it examines the conflicts and the violence that have marked the Colombian history, as well as the resistance and the resilience of the Colombian people. The third room is called "Art: Territory of Encounters and Disencounters", and it showcases the artistic expressions and movements that have emerged and developed in Colombia, as well as their influences and dialogues with other cultures and regions. The fourth room, "Society: Diversity and Difference," explores Colombia's social and cultural variety and complexity, as well as the problems and opportunities of coexistence in a diverse and democratic society.

The National Museum of Colombia Is a place where you can learn and appreciate the past and the present of Colombia, and where you can discover and enjoy its richness and its complexity. The museum also offers guided tours, audio guides, workshops, publications, and temporary exhibitions, to enhance your visit and learning. The museum is open from Tuesday to Saturday, from 9am to 6pm, and on Sundays, from 10 a.m. to 4 p.m. The entrance fee is 4,000 COP (1.14 USD) for adults, and free for children, students, and seniors. On Sundays, everyone can enter for free. The museum also has a shop, a restaurant, and a library.

THE BOGOTÁ GRAFFITI TOUR

The Bogotá Graffiti Tour is one of the best ways to experience the street art and culture of Bogotá, Colombia. It is a walking tour that takes you to different neighborhoods and locations in the city, where you can see some of the most amazing and diverse graffiti and murals that decorate the walls and buildings. The Bogotá Graffiti Tour is not only a visual feast, but also an educational and insightful journey, that reveals the stories, the meanings, and the messages behind the art, and how they reflect the history, the politics, and the society of Bogotá and Colombia. The Bogotá Graffiti Tour also introduces you to some of the most famous and talented street artists in Bogotá, who have created their own styles, techniques, and motivations, and who have contributed to the development and recognition of the graffiti scene in Bogotá and beyond. The Bogotá Graffiti Tour is a place where you can appreciate the artistry and the creativity of the street artists, and where you can learn about their issues, their movements, and their expressions.

The Bogotá Graffiti Tour was started In 2011 by Christian Petersen, a Canadian street artist and journalist, who wanted to share his passion and knowledge about the graffiti culture in Bogotá. Since then, the tour has grown to include other guides, who are also street artists, graffiti writers, or muralists, who have firsthand experience and expertise in the field. The tour has also become one of the most popular and recommended tours in Bogotá, with thousands of visitors and positive reviews. The tour has also collaborated with local and international organizations, such as the United Nations, the British Council, and the Colombian Ministry of Culture, to promote and support the street art and culture in Bogotá.

The Bogotá Graffiti Tour Is a free walking tour that operates every day at 10 a.m. and 2 p.m., rain or shine. The tour lasts about 2.5 hours, and covers about 3 kilometers (1.9 miles) of walking. The tour starts at the Parque de los Periodistas, next to the Liberator monument, where you can find the guides with the blue umbrellas. The tour ends at the Plaza de la Concordia, where you can find the largest graffiti mural in Bogotá. The tour does not require a reservation, but it is recommended to book online to secure your spot. The tour is based on donations, so you can pay what you want or what you can at the end of the tour. The tour is also available in English and Spanish, and you can choose the language of your preference. The tour is suitable for all ages and fitness levels, but you should wear comfortable shoes and clothes, and bring water, sunscreen, and a camera.

The Bogotá Graffiti Tour Is a unique and unforgettable experience, that will show you a different and authentic side of Bogotá, and that will make you appreciate the street art and culture of the city. The tour will take you to see some of the best and most diverse graffiti and murals in Bogotá, and that will explain the meaning, the message, and the context behind them. The tour will also introduce you to some of the most famous and talented street artists in Bogotá, and their styles, techniques, and motivations. The tour will also teach you about the history, the politics, and the society of Bogotá and Colombia, and how they are reflected and expressed in street art. The tour will also inspire you to see the city with new eyes, and to discover the beauty and the creativity that lies in its walls and buildings.

Usaquén is one of the most charming and lovely neighborhoods in Bogotá, Colombia. It is located in the north of the city, and it is part of the first locality of Bogotá. Usaquén has about 502,000 residents and an elevation of 2,567 meters.

Usaquén was founded in 1539 by the Spanish conquistador Pedro de Alvarado, who named it after the indigenous chief Usaque, who ruled the area before the arrival of the Europeans. Usaquén was a separate town until 1954, when it was annexed to Bogotá. However, Usaquén still preserves its colonial and rural atmosphere, with its whitewashed houses, cobblestone streets, and green hills. Usaquén is also known for its cultural and gastronomic diversity, with a variety of attractions and activities for visitors and locals alike.

Some of the main attractions and activities in Usaquén are:

- **The Church of Santa Bárbara de Usaquén:** This is the oldest and most emblematic building in Usaquén, dating back to the 17th century. The church has a simple and elegant architecture, with a white façade, a red tile roof, and a bell tower. The church is located in the main square of Usaquén, where you can also find a fountain, a statue of Simón Bolívar, and a clock tower. The church is open from Monday to Sunday, from 6 a.m. to 8 p.m., and it offers mass services and cultural events.

- **The Plaza de Usaquén:** This is the heart and soul of Usaquén, where you can enjoy the lively and colorful atmosphere of the neighborhood. The plaza is surrounded by restaurants, cafes, bars, and shops, where you can taste the local and international cuisine, have a drink, or buy souvenirs. The plaza is also the venue for the Mercado de las Pulgas, or the flea market, which takes place every Sunday from 9 a.m. to 5 p.m. The flea market is a great place to find handicrafts, antiques, art, books, and food, as well as to enjoy live music, street performers, and cultural activities. The plaza is also decorated with lights and ornaments during the Christmas season, making it a festive and magical place to visit.

- **The Hacienda Santa Bárbara:** This is a former country estate that belonged to the aristocratic Peña family, who built it in the 19th century. The hacienda has a colonial style architecture, with a yellow façade, a red tile roof, and a large courtyard. The hacienda is now a shopping mall, where you can find a variety of stores, restaurants, cinemas, and services. The hacienda also has a chapel, a museum, and a park, where you can learn more about the history and the culture of Usaquén. The hacienda is open from Monday to Sunday, from 10 a.m. to 9 p.m.

Usaquén is a neighborhood that offers a unique and cozy experience in Bogotá, where you can enjoy the charm and the beauty of the colonial and rural heritage, as well as the diversity and the quality of the modern and urban life. Usaquén is a place where you can escape the hustle and bustle of Bogotá, and where you can relax and have a good time.

SALT CATHEDRAL OF ZIPAQUIRA

The Salt Cathedral of Zipaquira is one of the most unique and spectacular attractions in Bogotá, Colombia. It is located in the town of Zipaquira, about 50 kilometers (31 miles) north of Bogotá, at an altitude of 2,652 meters (8,701 feet). The Salt Cathedral of Zipaquira is part of a larger complex called the Salt Park, which also includes a museum, a spa, and a restaurant.

The Salt Cathedral of Zipaquira was built Inside a salt mine that has been exploited since pre-Columbian times by the Muisca people and later by the Spanish colonizers. The salt mine has a rich historical and cultural significance since it was a source of riches and power for the region, as well as the inspiration for the tale of El Dorado, the legendary city of gold. The salt mine has also been a place of worship and devotion for the miners, who carved a small chapel in one of the tunnels in 1932. In 1954, a larger cathedral was inaugurated, but it was closed in 1990 due to safety issues. In 1995, a new cathedral was opened, deeper and safer than the previous one, and designed by the Colombian architect Roswell Garavito Pearl. The new cathedral is considered a masterpiece of engineering and art, and a symbol of the faith and the creativity of the Colombian people.

The Salt Cathedral of Zipaquira Is a subterranean church that is 180 meters (590 feet) below the surface, and that covers an area of 8,500 square meters (91,493 square feet). The cathedral has a series of chambers, tunnels, and sculptures that are made of salt and that represent the main stages of the Christian faith, such as the stations of the cross, the birth of Jesus, and the creation of the world. The cathedral also has a dome, a nave, and an altar, that are illuminated by colorful lights and that create a mystical and spiritual atmosphere. The cathedral can accommodate up to 8,400 people, and it offers mass services and cultural events. The cathedral also has a choir, an organ, and a sound system, that enhance the acoustics and the music of the place. The cathedral is also a natural reserve, where you can enjoy the flora and fauna of the Andean forest.

The Salt Cathedral of Zipaquira Is a place where you can admire the beauty and the ingenuity of Bogotá, and where you can feel the awe and the faith of Bogotá. The cathedral is a tourist destination and a place of pilgrimage in the country, and it has received several awards and recognitions, such as the First Wonder of Colombia in 2007, and the Guinness World Record for the largest underground cross in 2010. The cathedral is open from Monday to Sunday, from 9 a.m. to 6 p.m. The entrance fee is 60,000 COP (17 USD) for adults, and 35,000 COP (10 USD) for children, students, and seniors. The entrance fee includes a guided tour, an audio guide, and access to the Salt Park. You can also book a private tour, a VIP tour, or a night tour, for an additional cost.

SIMON BOLIVAR PARK

Simon Bolivar Park is the largest and most popular park in Bogotá, Colombia. It is named after the Latin American Liberator Simón Bolívar, who led the independence movement against the Spanish Empire. The park is located in the locality of Teusaquillo, in the center of the city, and it is part of the cultural network of the Banco de la República, the central bank of Colombia.

Simon Bolivar Park has an area of 400 hectares (990 acres), which makes it bigger than the Central Park in New York. The park has a lake of 11 hectares (27 acres), where you can rent paddle boats or enjoy the view of the ducks and geese. The park also has a forest of 113 hectares (279 acres), where you can walk, bike, or picnic among the trees and flowers. The park also has a sports complex of 68 hectares (168 acres), where you can play soccer, tennis, basketball, volleyball, or skate. The park also has a concert venue of 37 hectares (91 acres), where you can attend music festivals, cultural events, or shows. The park also has a flag square of 7 hectares (17 acres), where you can see the flags of the countries that Simón Bolívar liberated.

Simon Bolivar Park also has many attractions and activities for all ages and tastes. Some of the main attractions are:

- **The Botanical Garden José Celestino Mutis:** This is the largest botanical garden in Colombia, and it has more than 19,000 plants of 5,000 species, from different regions and ecosystems of the country. The botanical garden also has a butterfly house, an orchid house, a cactus house, and a medicinal plants house. The botanical garden also has a museum, a library, and a restaurant. The botanical garden is open from Tuesday to Sunday, from 8 a.m. to 5 p.m. The entrance fee is 3,500 COP (1 USD) for adults, and 1,800 COP (0.5 USD) for children, students, and seniors.

- **The Children's Museum of Bogotá:** This is a museum that aims to stimulate the curiosity, creativity, and learning of children, through interactive and playful exhibits. The museum has 22 rooms, where children can explore topics such as science, art, technology, culture, and society. The museum also has a planetarium, a theater, and a cafeteria. The museum is open from 9 in the morning to 5 p.m. on Tuesdays through Fridays and from 10 in the morning to 6 p.m. on Saturdays, Sundays, and holidays. The entrance fee is 12,000 COP (3.4 USD) for adults, and 10,000 COP (2.8 USD) for children. [4](^5^) ![Children's Museum of Bogotá]

- **The Salitre Mágico:** This is an amusement park that has more than 40 attractions, such as roller coasters, carousels, bumper cars, and water slides. The park also has shows, games, and food stalls. The park is open from Wednesday to Sunday, and on holidays, from 10 a.m. to 6 p.m. The entrance fee is 25,000 COP (7.1 USD) for adults, and 20,000 COP (5.7 USD) for children. The entrance fee includes unlimited access to all the attractions, except for the go-karts and the bungee jumping.

- **The Mundo Aventura:** This is another amusement park that has more than 30 attractions, such as Ferris wheels, swings, trains, and boats. The park also has a zoo, where you can see animals such as lions, tigers, bears, and monkeys. The park also has shows, games, and food stalls. The park is open from Wednesday to Sunday, and on holidays, from 10 a.m. to 6 p.m. The entrance fee is 5,000 COP (1.4 USD) for adults, and 3,000 COP (0.9 USD) for children. The entrance fee does not include access to the attractions, which have different prices, ranging from 2,000 COP (0.6 USD) to 10,000 COP (2.8 USD).

- **The Parque de los Novios:** This is a water park that has pools, slides, fountains, and jacuzzis. The park also has a spa, where you can enjoy massages, sauna, and steam. The park also has a restaurant, a bar, and a disco. The park is open from Wednesday to Sunday, and on holidays, from 9 a.m. to 5 p.m. The entrance fee is 25,000 COP (7.1 USD) for adults, and 20,000 COP (5.7 USD) for children. The entrance fee includes access to all the facilities, except for the spa, which has an additional cost.

- **The Club de Golf El Salitre**: This is a golf club that has an 18-hole course, a driving range, a putting green, and a chipping area. The club also has a clubhouse, a restaurant, a bar, and a pro shop. The club is open from Tuesday to Sunday, from 6 a.m. to 6 p.m. The entrance fee is 80,000 COP (22.7 USD) for adults, and 40,000 COP (11.4 USD) for children. The entrance fee includes the green fee, the caddy fee, and the insurance.

The club also offers golf lessons, equipment rental, and tournaments.

Simon Bolivar Park is a place where you can breathe some fresh air, do some exercise, have some entertainment, or attend some events. The park is one of the most fun and enjoyable places in Bogotá, and it has something for everyone. The park is open every day, from 6 a.m. to 6 in the evening, and entry is free. The park also has a bike path, a skate park, a dog park, and a picnic area. The park also hosts several events throughout the year, such as the Summer Festival, the Rock to the Park Festival, the Jazz to the Park Festival, and the Christmas Lights Festival.

3

BOGOTÁ FOOD AND DRINK: THE TASTE OF BOGOTÁ

THE BEST RESTAURANTS AND CAFES IN BOGOTÁ

Bogotá has a lot of restaurants and cafes that offer a range of cuisines, from the local to the international, from the traditional to the modern, from the cheap to the expensive. You can find restaurants and cafes for every occasion, mood, and palate, and enjoy a delicious meal or a hot drink. Here are some of the best restaurants and cafes in Bogotá, and why I like them:

- **LEO**: This is one of the most prestigious and innovative restaurants in Bogotá, and one of the best in Latin America. Leo is run by the famous chef Leonor Espinosa, who is known for her creative and experimental cuisine, that showcases the diversity and richness of the Colombian ingredients and cultures. Leo has a tasting menu, that changes every season, and that takes you on a gastronomic journey through the different regions, ecosystems, and traditions of Colombia. Leo also has a wine cellar, a cocktail bar, and a live music show, that complement the dining experience. Leo is a place where you can have a memorable and exquisite meal

- **LA PUERTA FALSA:** This is one of the oldest and most traditional restaurants in Bogotá, and one of the most cozy and charming. La Puerta Falsa is located in La Candelaria, and has been serving the typical dishes of Bogotá since 1816. La Puerta Falsa has a simple and rustic décor, and a friendly and warm service. La Puerta Falsa is famous for its ajiaco, its tamales, its chocolate con queso, and its almojabanas, among other delicacies. Make sure to go to La Puerta Falsa, where you can have a satisfying and comforting meal.

ANDRES CARNE DE RES: This is one of the most fun and popular restaurants in Bogotá, and one of the most unique and crazy. Andres Carne de Res is located in Chia, a town about 30 minutes away from Bogotá, and has a huge and eclectic space that is decorated with thousands of objects, colors, and lights. It's where you can have a lot of fun and excitement.

Andres Carne de Res is famous for its meat, its salads, its drinks, and its desserts, among other dishes. Andres Carne de Res is also famous for its music, its dance, its shows, and its parties that last until the early morning.

SALVO PATRIA: This is one of the most trendy and hip restaurants in Bogotá, and one of the most delicious and healthy. Salvo Patria is located in Chapinero, and has a modern and minimalist décor, and a relaxed and cool service. Salvo Patria is known for its organic and local cuisine, that uses fresh and seasonal ingredients, and that mixes Colombian and Mediterranean flavors. Salvo Patria has a menu that changes every day, and that offers dishes like ceviche, pasta, salad, and steak, among others. Salvo Patria also has a bakery, a coffee shop, and a bookstore, that offer more options for eating and drinking.

- CREPES AND WAFFLES: This is one of the most affordable and popular restaurants in Bogotá, and one of the most sweet and savory. Crepes and Waffles is a chain of restaurants, that has many locations in Bogotá and other cities, and that has a casual and cheerful atmosphere. Crepes and Waffles is famous for its crepes and waffles, that can be filled with cheese, meat, vegetables, fruits, ice cream, chocolate, or anything you want. It also serves salads, soups, sandwiches, and juices, among other options. Crepes and Waffles is a place where you can enjoy variety and have a tasty and affordable meal.

These are just some of the best restaurants and cafes in Bogotá, but there are many more to discover and enjoy, you'll never run out of options.

Bogotá has a lot of bars and clubs that offer a range of drinks, music, and vibes, from the local to the international, from the traditional to the modern, from the cheap to the expensive. You can find bars and clubs for every taste, style, and mood, and enjoy a drink, a dance, or a chat. Here are some of the best bars and clubs in Bogotá, and why I like them:

ARMANDO RECORDS: This is one of the most cool and popular bars and clubs in Bogotá, and one of the best places to listen to live music. Armando Records is located in Zona Rosa, and has a rooftop terrace, a dance floor, and a concert hall, that offer different genres and atmospheres. Armando Records is famous for its indie, rock, and electronic music, and for hosting local and international bands and DJs. Armando Records is a place where you can enjoy the music and the view of Bogotá, and where you can have a fun and lively night.

GAIRA CAFÉ: This is one of the most authentic and traditional bars and clubs in Bogotá, and one of the best places to listen to Colombian music. Gaira Café is located in Zona G, and is owned by the famous singer Carlos Vives, who is known for his vallenato, cumbia, and pop music. Gaira Café has a restaurant, a bar, and a stage that offer different flavors and rhythms. Gaira Café is famous for its live shows that feature Carlos Vives and other Colombian artists, and for its tropical and festive vibe. You can enjoy the culture and the joy of Bogotá, and have a memorable and colorful night.

THEATRON: This is one of the most fun and inclusive bars and clubs in Bogotá, and one of the best places to celebrate diversity and tolerance. Theatron is located in Chapinero, and is the largest gay club in Latin America, and one of the largest in the world. Theatron has 13 rooms that offer different themes, music, and shows, from salsa to techno, from drag to cabaret. Theatron is famous for its open bar, its foam party, and its massive crowd that can reach up to 8,000 people. In case you're looking for a wild and crazy night, Theatron is the place.

LA VILLA: This is one of the most trendy and hip bars and clubs in Bogotá, and one of the best places to meet new people and have a good time. La Villa is located in Zona T, and has a cozy and rustic décor, and a friendly and lively service. The place is known for its international music, its karaoke nights, and its beer pong tournaments. You can enjoy the vibe and have a casual and cool night.

VIDEO CLUB: This is one of the most original and creative bars and clubs in Bogotá, and one of the best places to watch and dance to music videos. Video Club is located in San Felipe, and has a retro and futuristic décor, and a professional and enthusiastic service. The club is famous for its video screens, that play music videos from different genres and eras, and that sync with the sound system and the lights. Video Club is a place where you can enjoy the music and the visuals of Bogotá, and have a nostalgic and innovative night.

These are just some of the best bars and clubs in Bogotá, but there are many more to find and enjoy.

Bogotá has a nightlife and entertainment that never stops, and that offers a lot of fun and excitement for everyone. The city has a lot of options for nightlife and entertainment - live music and theater, comedy and cinema, festivals and events. You can find nightlife and entertainment for every interest, preference, and occasion, and enjoy a show, a laugh, or a party. Here are some of the nightlife and entertainment options in Bogotá, and some of my personal stories and recommendations:

-   **Live Music And Theater:** Bogotá has a lot of venues and stages that offer live music and theater. One of the best places to enjoy live music and theater in Bogotá is the Teatro Mayor Julio Mario Santo Domingo, a modern and impressive theater that hosts some of the best shows and performances in Bogotá. I remember going to see the musical Les Miserables there, and being amazed by the production, the talent, and the emotion.

- **Comedy And Cinema**: in Bogotá, you can find comedy and cinema for every taste and humor, from stand-up and improv, to sketch and sitcom, to drama and horror. You can also find comedy and cinema for every language and subtitle; Spanish, English, French, German, Portuguese and Italian. One of the best places to enjoy comedy and cinema in Bogotá is the Cine Tonala. I went once to see the movie Parasite there, and was surprised by the plot, the direction, and the message. Cine Tonala is a cozy and eclectic theater, that has a bar, a restaurant, and a shop, and that shows some of the best movies and comedians in Bogotá.

- **Festivals and Events:** Bogotá has a lot of festivals and events that offer a lot of culture and entertainment, from the local and the regional, to the national and the international. You can find festivals and events for every theme and occasion. I remember going to Rock al Parque to see the band Foo Fighters there. I was quite very much thrilled by the energy, by the crowd, and the sound. Rock al Parque is surely one of the best festivals and events in Bogotá. It's a free and massive music festival that takes place every year in the Simon Bolivar Park, and that features some of the best rock bands and artists in Bogotá and beyond.

4

BOGOTÁ CULTURE AND ARTS: THE SOUL OF BOGOTÁ

Bogotá is full of culture and arts that reflect its soul and its diversity. Bogotá has a lot of music and dance, art and literature, festivals and celebrations, theaters, museums, and galleries that offer a glimpse of its history, identity, and creativity. Bogotá also has a lot of people and customs that show its warmth, hospitality, and humor. I'll tell you about the culture and arts of Bogotá.

THE MUSIC AND DANCE

Bogotá has a lot of music and dance that express rhythm and passion. Bogotá has a variety of genres and styles, from the traditional and the folkloric, to the modern and the urban, from the local and the regional, to the national and the international. You can find music and dance for every taste and mood, from rock and jazz, to salsa and cumbia, to reggaeton and hip hop. You can also find music and dance for every occasion and place, from concerts and festivals, to bars and clubs, to parks and streets.

- **ROCK**: This is one of the most popular and influential genres in Bogotá. Rock has a long and strong tradition in Bogotá, and has produced some of the most famous and talented bands and artists in Colombia, such as Aterciopelados, Kraken, and Juanes. Rock also has a large and loyal fan base in Bogotá, and has some of the best venues and events in Bogotá, such as the Rock al Parque, the largest free rock festival in Latin America. Rock is a genre that I love, and that I always listen to.

- **SALSA**: This is one of the most fun and festive genres in Bogotá. Salsa has a rich and diverse history in Bogotá, and has been influenced by the Cuban, Puerto Rican, and Colombian styles. Salsa also has a vibrant and lively scene in Bogotá, and has some of the best schools and clubs in Bogotá, such as the Galeria Café Libro, the Quiebra Canto, and the El Goce Pagano.

- **REGGAETON**: This is one of the most trendy and modern genres in Bogotá, and one of the best ways to enjoy the urban and the global of Bogotá. Reggaeton has a recent and dynamic history in Bogotá, and has been influenced by the Jamaican, Panamanian, and Puerto Rican styles. Reggaeton also has a huge and young audience in Bogotá, and has some of the best stars and hits in Bogotá, such as J Balvin, Karol G, and Maluma.

These are just some of the music and dance of Bogotá, but there are many more to discover and enjoy and you'll never get tired of them.

THE ART AND LITERATURE OF BOGOTÁ

Bogotá boasts a variety of genres and styles, encompassing the traditional and realistic, the contemporary and abstract, the regional and national, and the worldwide and universal. You can find art and literature for every taste and interest, from painting and sculpture, to poetry and novels, to graffiti and comics. You can also find art and literature for inspiration.

- **FERNANDO BOTERO:** This is one of the most famous and influential artists in Bogotá, and one of the best representatives of Colombian art. Fernando Botero is known for his paintings and sculptures of exaggerated and voluptuous figures that reflect his style and his vision of the world. Fernando Botero also has a social and political critique in his works, that denounce the violence, the corruption, and the inequality in Colombia and beyond. Fernando Botero has a museum in Bogotá, that has more than 200 works of art, donated by him, and that showcase his talent and his generosity.

- **GABRIEL GARCIA MARQUEZ**: This is one of the most renowned and beloved writers in Bogotá, and one of the best examples of Latin American literature. Gabriel Garcia Marquez is known for his novels and stories of magical realism, that blend reality and fantasy, and that create a unique and captivating world. Gabriel Garcia Marquez also has a human and universal appeal in his works that explore the themes of love, death, memory, and identity. Gabriel Garcia Marquez has a cultural center in Bogotá, that has a library, a gallery, and a café, and that promotes his legacy and his influence.

- **BOGOTÁ GRAFFITI**: This is one of the most original and creative expressions of art and literature in Bogotá, and one of the best ways to discover the urban and the social of Bogotá. Bogotá Graffiti is a collective and diverse movement that uses the walls and the streets as a canvas and a medium, and that produces some of the best graffiti and murals in the world. Bogotá Graffiti also has a meaning and a message in its works, that reflect the issues, the movements, and the expressions of Bogotá and its people. Bogotá Graffiti has a tour in Bogotá, that takes you to see some of the best graffiti and murals in the city, and that explains the context and the story behind them.

THE FESTIVALS AND CELEBRATIONS

Bogotá has a lot of festivals and celebrations that express its culture and its joy. It has a variety of themes and occasions, and you can find festivals and celebrations for every season and date. You can also find festivals and celebrations for every genre and style, from rock and jazz, to salsa and cumbia, to classical and opera. Here are some of the festivals and celebrations of Bogotá, and why I like them:

- **ROCK AL PARQUE:** This is one of the most fun and popular festivals in Bogotá, and one of the best places to listen to live music. Rock al Parque is a free and massive music festival that takes place every year in the Simon Bolivar Park, and that features some of the best rock bands and artists in Bogotá and beyond. Rock al Parque also has a lot of activities and attractions, such as workshops, exhibitions, and food trucks.

- **BOGOTÁ BEER FESTIVAL**: This is one of the most delicious and festive festivals in Bogotá, and one of the best places to taste and drink beer. Bogotá Beer Festival is a gastronomic and cultural festival that takes place every year in different locations in Bogotá, and that showcases some of the best craft and artisanal beers in Bogotá and Colombia. Bogotá Beer Festival also has a lot of entertainment and fun, such as music, games, and contests.

BOGOTÁ BOOK FAIR: This is one of the best places to read and buy books in Bogotá. Bogotá Book Fair is a literary and academic festival that takes place every year in the Corferias, and that features some of the best authors and publishers in Bogotá and the world. Bogotá Book Fair also has a lot of events

71

and activities, such as lectures, workshops, and signings. Bogotá Book Fair is a festival that I admire, and I always visit as a book fan.

THE BEST THEATERS, MUSEUMS, AND GALLERIES IN BOGOTÁ

Bogotá has a lot of theaters, museums, and galleries that offer a lot of culture and entertainment, from the local and the regional, to the national and the international. You can find theaters, museums, and galleries for every interest and preference, from music and theater, to art and history, to science and technology. You can also find theaters, museums, and galleries for every budget and quality, from the free and the public, to the expensive and the private. Here are some of the best theaters, museums, and galleries in Bogotá:

- **TEATRO MAYOR JULIO MARIO SANTO DOMINGO**: This is one of the most modern and impressive theaters in Bogotá, and one of the best places to enjoy live music and theater. Teatro Mayor Julio Mario Santo Domingo is a cultural and artistic center that has two auditoriums that host some of the best shows and performances in Bogotá. Teatro Mayor Julio Mario Santo Domingo also has a library, a café, and a shop that offer more options for culture and entertainment. Teatro Mayor Julio Mario Santo Domingo is a theater that I like, and that I always go to when I want to see the best of Bogotá's culture and arts.

- **GOLD MUSEUM**: Again, this is one of the most impressive and important museums in Bogotá, and one of the best places to learn about the history and the diversity of Colombia. I have already talked about this museum in chapter 2, but the museum is worth being talked of again. The Gold Museum showcases the craftsmanship, the symbolism, and the spirituality of the ancient civilizations of Colombia, and their relationship with nature and the cosmos. The Gold Museum also has a room where you can experience a ritual of light and sound that recreates the ceremony of the offering of gold to the gods.

5

BOGOTÁ SHOPPING AND MARKETS: THE TREASURES OF BOGOTÁ

Bogotá is full of shopping and markets that offer the treasures and the bargains of Bogotá. Bogotá has a lot of places to buy souvenirs, handicrafts, clothes, and more, from the traditional and the authentic, to the modern and the fashionable, from the cheap and the local, to the expensive and the international. Bogotá also has a lot of markets and fairs, that offer a lot of products, prices, and bargaining skills, from the fresh and the organic, to the antique and the artistic, to the festive and the cultural. I'll tell you about the shopping and markets of Bogotá, and share with you some of my personal stories and recommendations.

The best places to buy souvenirs, handicrafts, clothes, and more

- LA CANDELARIA:

This is one of the most charming and historic neighborhoods in Bogotá, and one of the best places to buy souvenirs and handicrafts. La Candelaria is full of small and quaint shops that sell a variety of items, such as pottery, jewelry, textiles, paintings, and coffee. La Candelaria is also full of street vendors that sell more items, such as hats, bags, scarves, and magnets. La Candelaria is a place where you can find the most authentic and original souvenirs and handicrafts, and where you can support the local artisans and producers. La

Candelaria is a place that I love, and that I always visit when I want to buy something special and unique for myself or for my friends.

- **ZONA ROSA:** This is one of the most fashionable and luxurious neighborhoods in Bogotá, and one of the best places to buy clothes and more. Zona Rosa is full of large and modern malls, such as Andino, Atlantis, and El Retiro, that have a variety of stores, such as Zara, H&M, Nike, and Apple. Zona Rosa is also full of chic and exclusive boutiques, such as Carolina Herrera, Hugo Boss, and Louis Vuitton. Zona Rosa is a place where you can find the most trendy and stylish clothes and more, and where you can splurge and treat yourself. Zona Rosa is a place that I like, and that I always go to when I want to buy something new and fashionable for myself or for my family.

- **USAQUEN:** This is one of the most cozy and charming neighborhoods in Bogotá, and one of the best places to buy antiques and more. Usaquen is full of small and rustic shops that sell a variety of items, such as furniture, books, records, and toys. Usaquen is also full of flea markets and fairs, that take place every Sunday and holiday, and that offer more items, such as lamps, clocks, cameras, and dolls. Usaquen is a place where you can find the most vintage and nostalgic antiques and more, and where you can bargain and haggle.

These are just some of the best places to buy souvenirs, handicrafts, clothes, and more in Bogotá, but there are many more to discover and enjoy. Bogotá has a place to buy souvenirs, handicrafts, clothes, and more for every taste and budget, and you'll never run out of options.

THE BEST MARKETS AND FAIRS IN BOGOTÁ

- **PALOQUEMAO**: This is one of the most traditional and famous markets in Bogotá, and one of the best places to buy fresh and organic food. Paloquemao is a large and colorful market that has hundreds of stalls that sell a variety of products, such as fruits, vegetables, flowers, meat, cheese, and bread. Paloquemao is also a place where you can taste and try some of the typical dishes and drinks of Bogotá, such as ajiaco, tamal, and chocolate. Paloquemao is a market I always visit when I want to buy something fresh and delicious for myself or for my kitchen.

- **SAN ALEJO**: This is one of the most original and interesting markets in Bogotá, and one of the best places to buy antique and artistic items. San Alejo is a flea market that takes place every first and third Saturday of the month, in the Parque de la Independencia, and that has dozens of stalls that sell a variety of items, such as jewelry, books, records, and toys. San Alejo is also a place where you can find and buy some of the most unique and rare items, such as stamps, coins, cameras, and dolls.

- **AL PARQUE**: This is one of the most fun and festive fairs in Bogotá, and one of the best places to enjoy music and culture. Al Parque is a series of free and massive music festivals that take place every year in different parks of Bogotá, and that feature some of the best music genres and artists in Bogotá and beyond. Al Parque also has a lot of activities and attractions, such as workshops, exhibitions, and food trucks. Al Parque has different editions, such as Rock al Parque, Jazz al Parque, Salsa al Parque, and Hip Hop al Parque. These are just some of the best markets and fairs in Bogotá, but there are many more to discover and enjoy. Bogotá has a market and a fair for every interest and occasion, and you'll never get bored of them.

THE PRODUCTS, PRICES, AND BARGAINING SKILLS

Bogotá has a range of products, from the local and the regional, to the national and the international, from the cheap and the local, to the expensive and the international. You can find products for every need and want, from food and drink, to clothes and accessories, to souvenirs and gifts. Bogotá also has a range of prices, from the low and the affordable, to the high and the exclusive, from the fixed and the clear, to the negotiable and the flexible.

Some of the tips and tricks to have a safe and enjoyable shopping experience in Bogotá, and to avoid scams and rip-offs are:

- Know the currency and the exchange rate: Bogotá uses the Colombian peso as its currency, and the exchange rate varies depending on the market and the time. You can check the current exchange rate online, or at a bank or a currency exchange office. You can also use a calculator or an app to convert the prices to your own currency, and to compare the prices of different products and places. You should avoid exchanging money on the street, or at places that offer too good to be true rates, as they may be fraudulent or illegal. You should also avoid carrying too much cash, or showing it in public, as you may attract thieves or scammers. You should also have some coins and small bills, as some places may not have change, or may charge you extra for using large bills.

- Know the average prices and the quality standards: Bogotá has a wide range of prices and quality standards, depending on the product, the place, and the season. You can research the average prices and the quality standards online, or by asking locals or other travelers. You can also compare the prices and the quality of different products and places, and look for signs of quality, such as labels, certificates, or reviews. You should avoid buying products that are too cheap or too expensive, or that have no quality guarantees, as they may be fake, defective, or stolen. You should also avoid buying products that are illegal, prohibited, or endangered, such as drugs, weapons, or wildlife, as you may face legal consequences or ethical issues.

- Know the bargaining etiquette and the negotiation tactics: Bogotá has a culture of bargaining and negotiation, especially in markets and fairs, where the prices are not fixed, and where you can haggle and bargain for a better deal. You can learn the bargaining etiquette and the negotiation tactics online, or by observing locals or other travelers. You can also practice your bargaining skills and your negotiation tactics, and use some strategies, such as asking for a discount, offering a lower price, walking away, or buying in bulk. You should avoid being too aggressive or too passive, or being too rude or too polite, as you may offend or annoy the seller, or lose the deal. You should also avoid being too gullible or too suspicious, or being too eager or too indifferent, as you may fall for a scam or miss a bargain.

6

BOGOTÁ NATURE AND SPORTS: THE GREEN AND ACTIVE SIDE OF BOGOTÁ

Bogotá has a lot of places to hike, bike, raft, or zip-line that offer a lot of adventure and fun, from the mountains and the forests, to the rivers and the valleys, to the parks and the trails.

The best places to hike, bike, raft, or zip-line in Bogotá

Bogotá has a lot of places to hike, bike, raft, or zip-line that offer a lot of adventure and fun, from the mountains and the forests, to the rivers and the valleys, to the parks and the trails. Bogotá has a variety of places to hike, bike, raft, or zip-line, from the easy and the accessible, to the hard and the challenging, from the short and the quick, to the long and the slow.

- **MONSERRATE**: This is one of the most iconic and famous places to hike in Bogotá, and one of the best places to enjoy the view and the altitude of Bogotá. Monserrate is a mountain that rises to 3,152 meters above sea level, and that has a church and a sanctuary on its summit, which are visited by pilgrims and tourists. Monserrate has a trail that starts from the base of the mountain, and that takes about an hour and a half to reach the top, depending on your pace and your fitness. Monserrate also has a cable car and a funicular that offer a faster and easier way to go up and down the mountain.

- **CICLOVIA**: This is one of the most popular and appreciated places to bike in Bogotá, and one of the best places to enjoy the urban and the social of Bogotá. Ciclovia is a program that takes place every Sunday and holiday, from 7 am to 2 pm, and that closes some of the main streets and avenues of Bogotá, to allow people to use them for biking, walking, running, or skating. Ciclovia has a network of more than 120 kilometers of routes, that cover different areas and neighborhoods of Bogotá, and that offer different attractions and services, such as parks, markets, and stages.

- **TOBIA**: This is one of the most adventurous and exciting places to raft or zip-line in Bogotá, and one of the best places to enjoy the water and the speed of Bogotá. Tobia is a town that is located about 90 kilometers from Bogotá, and that is surrounded by the Magdalena River and the Tobia River, that offer some of the best rapids and currents for rafting. Tobia also has a canopy park, that has more than 10 zip-lines, that cross the river and the forest, and that offer some of the best views and sensations for zip-lining.

FAUN AND FLOWER IN BOGOTÁ

- **FLOWERS**: Bogotá has a lot of flowers that offer a lot of color and fragrance; the roses and the orchids, the sunflowers and the daisies, to the carnations and the lilies. You can find flowers for every occasion and mood. Some of the flowers of Bogotá are:

- **ORCHIDS**: These are some of the most beautiful and diverse flowers in the world, and Colombia has more than 4,000 species of them, some of them endemic to the country. Bogotá has a special place for orchids, as it hosts the annual Orchid Fair, where you can see and buy some of the most stunning and unique orchids, such as the Odontoglossum lindenii, the national flower of Colombia. Bogotá also has the José Celestino Mutis Botanical Garden, where you can see and learn more about the orchids and other plants of Bogotá and Colombia.

- **ROSES**: These are some of the most popular and exported flowers in the world, and Colombia is one of the largest producers of them, with more than 6,000 hectares of rose plantations. Bogotá also has a lot of places where you can buy and enjoy roses, such as the Paloquemao market, where you can find roses of different sizes and prices, or the Usaquen flea market, where you can find roses of different shapes and colors.

These are just some of the flowers of Bogotá, but there are many more, you'll never get enough of them.

- **BIRDS:**

You can find birds for every interest and curiosity, from the scenic and the relaxing, to the educational and the cultural, to the thrilling and the exciting. Some of the birds of Bogotá are:

- Hummingbirds: These are some of the most amazing and diverse birds in the world, and Colombia has more than 165 species of them, some of them endemic to the country. Bogotá has a special place for hummingbirds, as it has the Observatorio de Colibries, where you can see and feed some of the most stunning and unique hummingbirds, such as the blue-throated starfrontlet, the glittering-throated emerald, and the rufous-tailed hummingbird. Bogotá also has the Parque La Florida, where you can see and hear more hummingbirds and other birds in their natural habitat.

- Toucans: These are some of the most colorful and charismatic birds in the world, and Colombia has more than 15 species of them, some of them endemic to the country. Bogotá has a lot of toucans that offer a lot of variety and personality, from the emerald toucanet and the keel-billed toucan, to the channel-billed toucan and the chestnut-mandibled toucan. Bogotá also has a lot of places where you can see and admire toucans, such as the Parque Jaime Duque, where you can find toucans and other animals in a zoo and a park, or the Parque Nacional Natural Chingaza, where you can find toucans and other wildlife in a reserve and a park.

- Turtles: These are some of the most ancient and diverse reptiles in the world, and Colombia has more than 30 species of them, some of them endemic to the country. Bogotá has a special place for turtles, as it has the Fundación Zoológica de Cali, where you can see and learn about some of the most fascinating and endangered turtles, such as the Magdalena river turtle, the giant Amazon river turtle, and the leatherback sea turtle. Bogotá also has the Parque Simón Bolívar, where you can see and feed more turtles and other animals in a lake and a park.

7

BOGOTÁ DAY TRIPS AND EXCURSIONS: THE PLACES TO EXPLORE AROUND BOGOTÁ

Bogotá is a wonderful city to visit, but sometimes you may want to explore the nearby attractions and enjoy the natural beauty and cultural diversity of the country. Here are some of the excursions that you can do from Bogotá, as well as the transportation options and suggested itineraries for each one:

VILLA DE LEYVA

This is one of the most charming and picturesque colonial towns in Colombia, and it is located about 160 kilometers (100 miles) north of Bogotá. Villa de Leyva is famous for its whitewashed houses, cobblestone streets, and large main square, where you can admire the historical buildings and monuments. Villa de Leyva is also surrounded by stunning landscapes, such as mountains, valleys, and deserts, where you can find archaeological sites, fossils, waterfalls, and vineyards. Villa de Leyva is a perfect place to relax and enjoy the tranquility and beauty of the countryside.

- **TRANSPORTATION**: The best way to get to Villa de Leyva from Bogotá is by bus, which takes about 3 to 4 hours and costs about 25,000 COP (7 USD) per person. You can take a bus from the Terminal de Transporte de Bogotá, located on Avenida Calle 57 with Carrera 69. You can also take a taxi or a private car, which takes about 2.5 hours and costs about 300,000 COP (85 USD) per car. You can also rent a car in Bogotá and drive to Villa de Leyva, but you should be careful with the traffic and the road conditions.

- **ITINERARY**

You can visit Villa de Leyva as a day trip from Bogotá, or you can stay overnight and enjoy more time in the town and the surroundings. Here is a suggested itinerary for a day trip from Bogotá:

- Depart from Bogotá early in the morning and arrive in Villa de Leyva around 10 a.m.
- Explore the town center and visit the main attractions, such as the Plaza Mayor, the Casa Museo Antonio Nariño, the Museo del Carmen, and the Iglesia de Nuestra Señora del Rosario.
- Have lunch at one of the many restaurants and cafes in the town, such as La Tienda de Teresa, El Solar de la Guaca, or La Galleta.

- In the afternoon, choose one of the following options to visit the nearby attractions:
- Option A: Visit the Museo Paleontológico, where you can see fossils of dinosaurs and other prehistoric animals, and the Pozos Azules, a series of turquoise pools in the desert.
- Option B: Visit the Convento del Santo Ecce Homo, a 17th-century monastery with a museum and a garden, and the Casa Terracota, a giant house made entirely of clay.
- Option C: Visit the Parque Arqueológico de Monquirá, where you can see ancient stone carvings and sculptures, and the Viñedo Ain Karim, where you can taste and buy local wines.
- Return to Bogotá in the evening and arrive around 8 p.m.

This is a small and scenic town near Bogotá, where you can visit the famous Lake Guatavita, the sacred site of the Muisca people and the origin of the legend of El Dorado. Lake Guatavita is a circular lake located in a crater, where the Muisca used to perform rituals and offerings of gold and precious stones to their god. The lake is also a natural reserve, where you can enjoy the flora and fauna of the Andean forest. Guatavita is a place where you can learn about the history and culture of the indigenous people of Colombia, as well as admire the beauty and mystery of the lake.

Transportation: The best way to get to Guatavita from Bogotá is by bus, which takes about 2 hours and costs about 15,000

COP (4 USD) per person. You can take a bus from the Portal del Norte Station of the TransMilenio, located on Avenida Calle 170 with Autopista Norte. You can also take a taxi or a private car, which takes about 1.5 hours and costs about 200,000 COP (57 USD) per car. You can also rent a car in Bogotá and drive to Guatavita, but you should be careful with the traffic and the road conditions.

- ITINERARY

You can visit Guatavita as a half-day trip from Bogotá, or you can combine it with other nearby attractions, such as Zipaquirá or Suesca. Here is a suggested itinerary for a half-day trip from Bogotá:

- Depart from Bogotá in the morning and arrive in Guatavita around 10 a.m.

- Explore the town center and visit the main attractions, such as the Plaza de los Artesanos, the Iglesia de Santa María de Guatavita, and the Mirador de Guatavita.

- Have a snack or a drink at one of the local cafes, such as Café de la Plaza, Café de la Montaña, or Café de la Cuchara.

- In the afternoon, take a taxi or a bus to Lake Guatavita, which is about 15 kilometers (9 miles) away from the town. You can also hike to the lake, which takes about 2 hours and offers beautiful views of the countryside.

- At the lake, you can take a guided tour that will explain the history, the legend, and the ecology of the place. You can also walk around the lake and enjoy the scenery and nature. The tour and the walk take about 2 hours in total.

- Return to Guatavita and then to Bogotá in the evening and arrive around 6 p.m.

CHICAQUE NATURAL PARK

This is one of the most beautiful and diverse places to explore around Bogotá, and one of the best places to enjoy the cloud forest. Chicaque Natural Park is a nature reserve that covers 300 hectares of land, and that has more than 10 kilometers of trails that take you through different ecosystems, such as the oak forest, the cloud forest, and the páramo. Chicaque Natural Park is also a place where you can see and learn about the flora and fauna of the region, such as the orchids, the ferns, the hummingbirds, and the monkeys. Chicaque Natural Park is also a place where you can have fun and adventure, as the park has a zip-line, a canopy, and a rappel, and as the park has a lookout point, a waterfall, and a lake. Chicaque Natural Park is a place where you can appreciate the beauty and the diversity of the cloud forest, and where you can feel the fresh and the humid air.

How to plan your itinerary and budget: The best way to get to Chicaque Natural Park is by taking a bus from the Terminal de Transporte de Bogotá to San Antonio del Tequendama, and then taking a taxi to the park entrance. The bus costs 7,000 COP (about $2 USD) per person, and the taxi costs 15,000 COP (about $4 USD) per ride. The park is open from 8am to 4pm, and the entrance fee is 20,000 COP (about $5 USD) per person. You can also rent a cabin or a tent at the park, if you want to stay overnight. The cabin costs 120,000 COP (about $32 USD) per night, and the tent costs 40,000 COP (about $11 USD) per night. You can also bring your own food and drinks, or buy them at the park's restaurant or store. For an extra charge, guided excursions are also available at the park. You can also book your trip online, through the park's website.

CHOACHI

This is one of the most relaxing and soothing places to explore around Bogotá, and one of the best places to enjoy the hot springs and waterfalls. Choachi is a town that is located about 50 kilometers from Bogotá, and that has a lot of natural attractions, such as the Termales de Santa Monica, the La Chorrera waterfall, and the Ubaque lagoon. Choachi is also a place where you can see and learn about the culture and history of the region, such as the Muisca people, the colonial architecture, and the local gastronomy. Choachi is also a place where you can have fun and adventure, as the town has a lot of activities, such as hiking, biking, horseback riding, and paragliding. Choachi is a place where you can appreciate the beauty and the tranquility of the hot springs and waterfalls, and where you can feel the warm and the healing water.

How To Plan Your Itinerary And Budget

The best way to get to Choachi is by taking a bus from the Portal 20 de Julio station of the TransMilenio system, or from the Terminal de Transporte de Bogotá, to Choachi. The bus costs 10,000 COP (about $3 USD) per person, and it takes about two hours. The town is open 24 hours a day, and there is no entrance fee. You can also rent a room or a cabin in the town, if you want to stay overnight. The room costs 60,000 COP (about $16 USD) per night, and the cabin costs 100,000 COP (about $27 USD) per night. You can also bring your own food and drinks, or buy them at the town's restaurants or stores. The town also offers tours and packages, for an additional fee. You can also book your trip online, through the town's website.

SUESCA

This is one of the most adventurous and exciting places to explore around Bogotá, and one of the best places to enjoy the rock climbing paradise. Suesca is a town that is located about 60 kilometers from Bogotá, and that has a lot of natural attractions, such as the Rocas de Suesca, the Laguna de

Suesca, and the Bosque de las Rocas. Suesca is also a place where you can see and learn about the culture and history of the region, such as the rock art, the colonial church, and the local crafts. Suesca is also a place where you can have fun and adventure, as the town has a lot of activities, such as rock climbing, bouldering, camping, and kayaking. Suesca is a place where you can appreciate the beauty and the challenge of the rock climbing paradise, and where you can feel the adrenaline and the satisfaction.

How To Plan Your Itinerary And Budget

The best way to get to Suesca is by taking a bus from the Portal Norte station of the TransMilenio system, or from the Terminal de Transporte de Bogotá, to Suesca. The bus costs 8,000 COP (about $2 USD) per person, and it takes about an hour and a half. The town is open 24 hours a day, and there is no entrance fee. You can also rent a room or a tent in the town, if you want to stay overnight. The room costs 50,000 COP (about $13 USD) per night, and the tent costs 15,000 COP (about $4 USD) per night. You can also bring your own food and drinks, or buy them at the town's restaurants or stores. The town also offers equipment rental, guides, and courses, for an additional fee. You can also book your trip online, through the town's website.

8

BOGOTÁ OFF THE BEATEN PATH: THE HIDDEN AND UNUSUAL SPOTS IN BOGOTÁ

I always enjoy discovering new and fun things to do and see in Bogotá, that make me feel surprised and delighted, from the weird and the wonderful, to the spooky and the mysterious, to the artistic and the creative. I also love finding new and beautiful places to enjoy the views, the sunsets, and the stars in Bogotá, that make me feel relaxed and inspired.

THE QUIRKY AND FUN THIN'S TO DO AND SEE IN BOGOTÁ

Bogotá has a lot of quirky and fun things to do and see, that make me feel like a kid again, or like a detective, or like an artist. Bogotá has a lot of things to do and see that are different and original, including museums, galleries, parks and monuments. You can find things to do and see that are suitable for every taste and mood, from the humorous and the playful, to the scary and the thrilling, to the educational and the cultural. Here are some of the quirky and fun things to do and see in Bogotá, and why I like them:

MUSEO DEL CHICÓ

This is one of the most unexpected and amusing museums in Bogotá, and one of the best places to have a laugh and a smile in Bogotá. Museo del Chicó is a museum that displays the collection of Mercedes Sierra de Pérez, a wealthy and eccentric lady who lived in a mansion in the Chicó neighborhood, and who collected a lot of bizarre and curious items, such as dolls, masks, hats, and shoes. Museo del Chicó is also a place where you can have a picnic and a stroll in the gardens of the mansion, and where you can see some of the most hilarious and outrageous statues, such as a giant turtle, a fat lady, and a naked man. Museo del Chicó is a place that I always visit when I want to have a laugh and a smile in Bogotá.

CEMENTERIO CENTRAL

This is one of the most spooky and fascinating places in Bogotá, and one of the best places to have a chill and a thrill in Bogotá. Cementerio Central is a cemetery that dates back to 1836, and that hosts the graves of some of the most famous and infamous people in Colombia, such as presidents, writers, artists, and criminals. Cementerio Central is also a place where you can have a tour and a story in the night, and where you can hear some of the most scary and mysterious legends, such as the ghost of the widow, the curse of the vampire, and the secret of the mummy. Cementerio Central is a place that I always visit when I want to have a chill and a thrill in Bogotá.

GRAFFITI TOUR

This is one of the most artistic and creative things to do in Bogotá, and one of the best places to have a color and a culture in Bogotá. Graffiti Tour is a tour that takes you around the streets and walls of Bogotá, and that shows you some of the most stunning and meaningful graffiti and street art, that express the social and political issues, the history and the identity, and the dreams and the hopes of Bogotá and Colombia. Graffiti Tour is also a thing where you can have a guide and a lesson, and where you can learn more about the artists and the techniques, the messages and the symbols, and the challenges and the opportunities of graffiti and street art.

These are just some of the quirky and fun things to do and see in Bogotá, but there are many more to discover and enjoy. Bogotá always has things to do and see, and you'll never get bored of them.

THE BEST PLACES TO ENJOY THE VIEWS, THE SUNSETS, AND THE STARS.

Bogotá has a lot of places that offer a different perspective and atmosphere; the mountains and the hills, the parks and the lakes, to rooftops and terraces. You can find places that are suitable for every occasion and mood; romantic and cozy, social and lively, to peace and serenity. Here are some of the best places to enjoy the views, the sunsets, and the stars in Bogotá, and some insider tips from the locals:

MONSERRATE: This is one of the most iconic and spectacular places in Bogotá, and one of the best places to enjoy the views, the sunsets, and the stars in Bogotá. Monserrate is a mountain that rises to 3,152 meters above sea level, and that offers a stunning panoramic view of the city and the surrounding landscape. Monserrate is also a place where you can enjoy the sunset and the stars, as the sky changes colors and the city lights up. Monserrate is also a place where you can visit a colonial church, a sanctuary, and a market, and where you can have a meal or a drink at one of the restaurants or cafes. Monserrate is a place that I always visit when I want to enjoy the views, the sunsets, and the stars in Bogotá.

Insider tip: The best way to get to Monserrate is by taking the cable car or the funicular, which operate from 6am to 11:30 pm on weekdays, and from 5:30 am to 11:30 pm on weekends and holidays. The ticket costs 22,000 COP (about $6 USD) round-trip. You can also hike to Monserrate, which takes about an hour and a half, but it is only recommended during the day and with a local guide, as the trail can be steep and unsafe.

PARQUE DE LA 93: This is one of the most trendy and lively places in Bogotá, and one of the best places to enjoy the views, the sunsets, and the stars in Bogotá. Parque de la 93 is a park that is surrounded by restaurants, bars, cafes, and shops, and that offers a view of the modern and cosmopolitan side of the city. Parque de la 93 is also a place where you can enjoy the sunset and the stars, as the park hosts events, concerts, and festivals, and as the nightlife scene gets going. Parque de la 93 is also a place where you can relax and have fun, as the park has a playground, a fountain, and a chess board, and as the park is pet-friendly and family-friendly.

Insider tip: The best way to get to Parque de la 93 is by taking the TransMilenio bus to the Calle 100 station, and then walking for about 15 minutes along 15th avenue. You can also take a taxi or a bike, as the park has a bike parking area. There is no entry charge, and the park is open 24 hours a day. You can find a lot of options for dining and drinking around the park, whether local or international cuisine.

LA CALERA:

This is one of the most scenic and romantic places in Bogotá, and one of the best places to enjoy the views, the sunsets, and the stars in Bogotá. La Calera is a town that is located about 18 kilometers from Bogotá, and that offers a view of the rural and natural side of the city. La Calera is also a place where you can enjoy the sunset and the stars, as the town has a lookout point, a lake, and a park, and as the town has a clear and dark sky. La Calera is also a place where you can have a picnic or a barbecue, and where you can try the local specialty, the canelazo, a hot drink made with aguardiente, sugar, and cinnamon. La Calera is a place that I always visit when I want to enjoy the views, the sunsets, and the stars in Bogotá.

Insider tip: The best way to get to La Calera is by taking a taxi or a car, as the public transportation is limited and unreliable. The road to La Calera is winding and steep, so it is advisable to drive carefully and slowly. The lookout point is open from 6am to 10pm, and there is no entrance fee. You can find a lot of vendors selling food, drinks, and souvenirs along the road, but you can also bring your own snacks and beverages.

9

BOGOTÁ WRAP UP

Bogotá is a city that will captivate you with its diversity and complexity. It is a city that combines the old and the new, the traditional and the modern, the local and the global. It is a city that has a rich history and culture, as well as a vibrant and dynamic present and future. It is a city that has something for everyone, and that will surprise you with its beauty and its creativity.

In Bogotá, you can enjoy the cultural, historical, artistic, and gastronomic attractions of the city, such as the Gold Museum, the National Museum, the Botanical Garden, the Plaza de Bolívar, the La Candelaria neighborhood, the Monserrate hill, and the Usaquén district. You can also enjoy the nightlife, the music, and the party of the city, such as the Zona T, the Zona G, the Zona Rosa, the Armando Records, the Gaira Café, and the Bogotá Graffiti Tour. You can also explore the nearby attractions and enjoy the natural beauty and cultural diversity of the country, such as the Salt Cathedral of Zipaquira, the Villa de Leyva, the Guatavita Lake, and the Suesca Rocks.

Bogotá is a city that you will love and remember. It is a city that will make you feel at home, and that will make you want to come back. It is a city that will inspire you and challenge you. It is a city that will show you the best of Colombia, and the best of yourself.

I hope you enjoyed this travel guide about Bogotá, Colombia. I hope you found it useful and informative, I wish you a wonderful time in Bogotá, that you have a safe and happy journey.

MAPS
MAP SHOWING THE INTERNATIONAL AIRPORT AND MONSERRATE

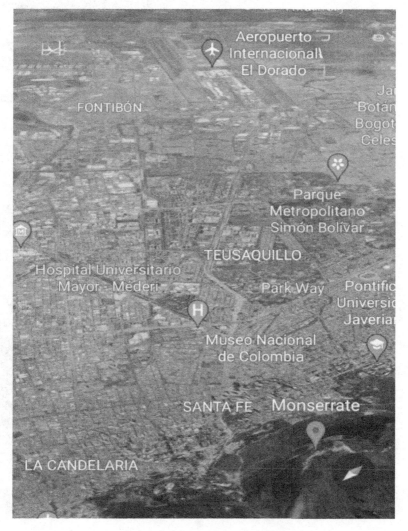

MAP SHOWING LA CANDELARIA

MAP SHOWING THE GOLD MUSEUM

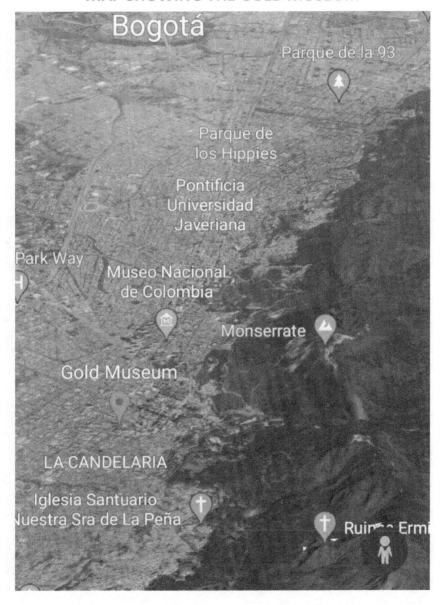

MAP SHOWING THE NATIONAL MUSEUM OF COLOMBIA

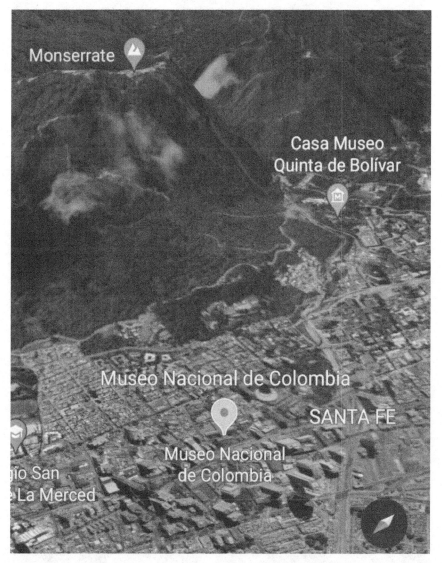

MAP SHOWING THE BOGOTÁ GRAFFITI TOUR

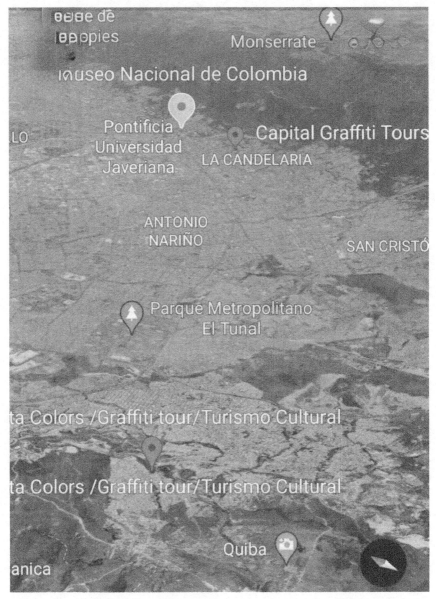

MAP SHOWING PLAZA DE BOLIVAR & PRESIDENTIAL VILLA

MAP SHOWING BOTERO MUSEUM

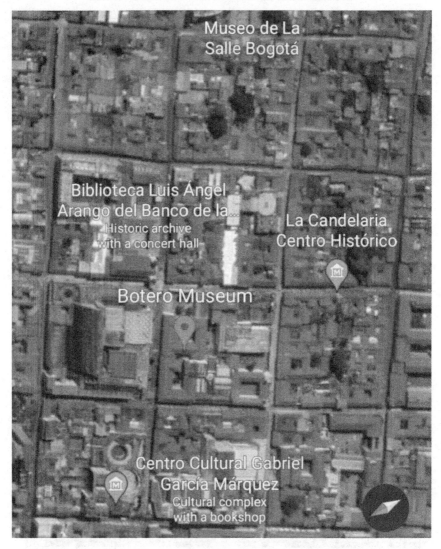

MAP SHOWING THE SALT CATHEDRAL

68890783R10066